I0477939

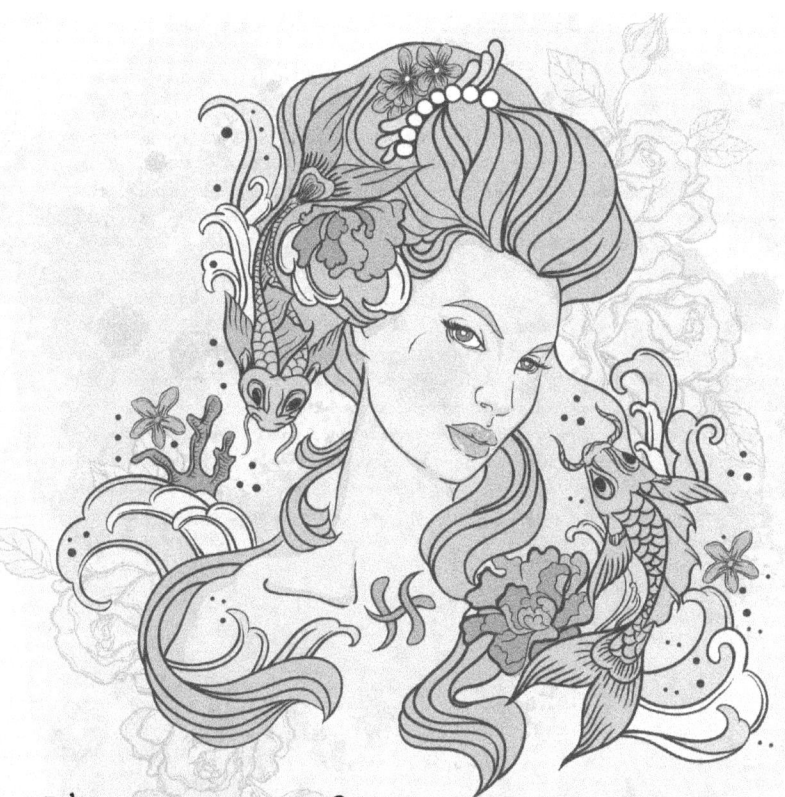

Flower Coloring Pages For Adults

30 Anti-Stress Pages For You

Color Your Day!

Vickie Granger

Introduction

Are you interested in relieving some of the stress accumulated throughout of the day? Do you want to unleash your inner creativity but you are unsure how? If your answer to either of these questions is yes, this adult coloring book is more than perfect for you. In just a matter of days, you will begin to feel more relaxed and at peace with yourself, re-discovering one of the greatest pleasures of your childhood: coloring.

Adult coloring is more than a trend, it represents an opportunity for you to unleash every creative fiber you have in your body. When you select colors and decide on how to fill the flower patterns, your brain is active and yet fully relaxed. Negative thoughts and emotions are eliminated and you will feel like a new person. You will smile, enjoying yourself and the activity you have recently discovered. A coloring book can be one of the most relaxing activities you have tried in your life, as you will have the opportunity to discover on your own.

There are no many things in life that are as entertaining an adult coloring book. We have chosen flower designs because these will allow you the best opportunity to activate your creative side. Use this book in order to relax after a hard day at the office or, in weekends, as an activity for the entire family. Do not hesitate to suggest this book to your friends and family members as well. Happy coloring!

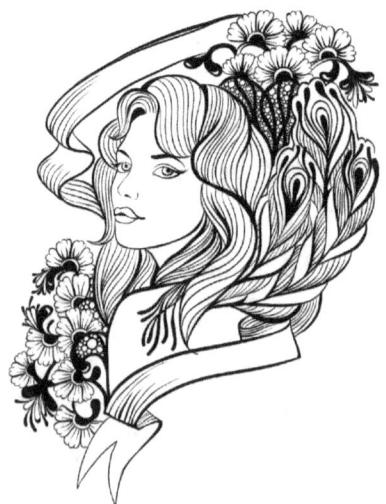

How to Use This Book

Given the fact that you haven't probably colored for more than twenty years, it is only normal that you are curious on finding out more information on its proper usage. However, the book should be used exactly as you believe; all you have to do is choose the desired colors and put your creativity to work. Do not worry about color combinations, as any color combo is good.

You can use this book anywhere you may find yourself, whether you are on a plane, taking a break at work or at home, looking for an afternoon pastime. You can listen to music in the background and have the time of your life. Or, if you want, you can share this experience with the rest of your family. As for the materials that you should use, it is recommended that you go with regular colored pencils. Gel pens are also a great alternative, the colors being more intense in this situation.

The more you will color, the better you will become (like anything in life). Just make sure that you work the edges first and then color in, as this will help you stay within the lines. Do not press too hard, as you will ruin the page. Moreover, this activity should be about relaxation and pressing hard on the page will have the opposite effect. And, most importantly, you should have fun. This is what an adult coloring book is all about, unleashing the child you have still hidden inside. Enjoy!

All pictures used in this book, including the cover picture are sourced from shutterstock.com

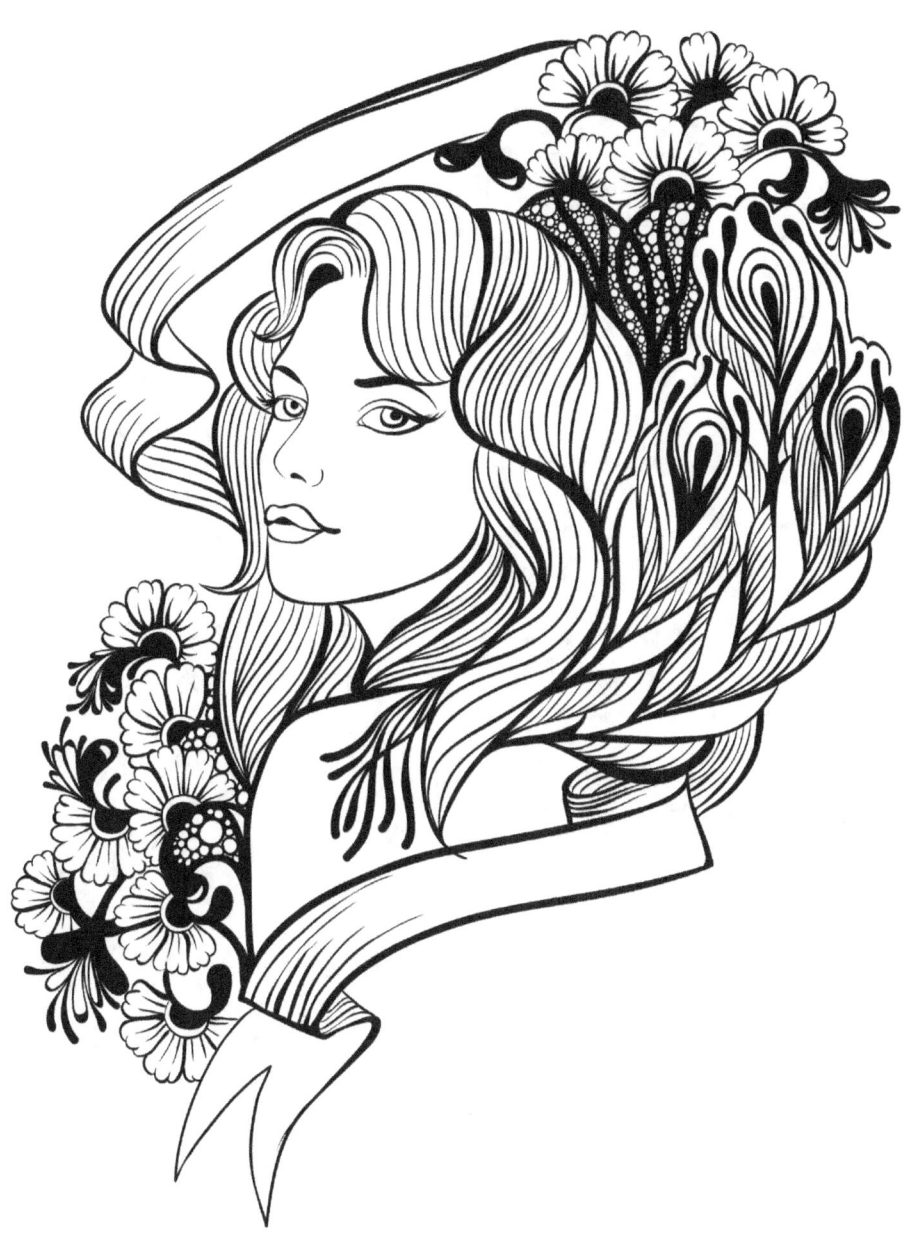

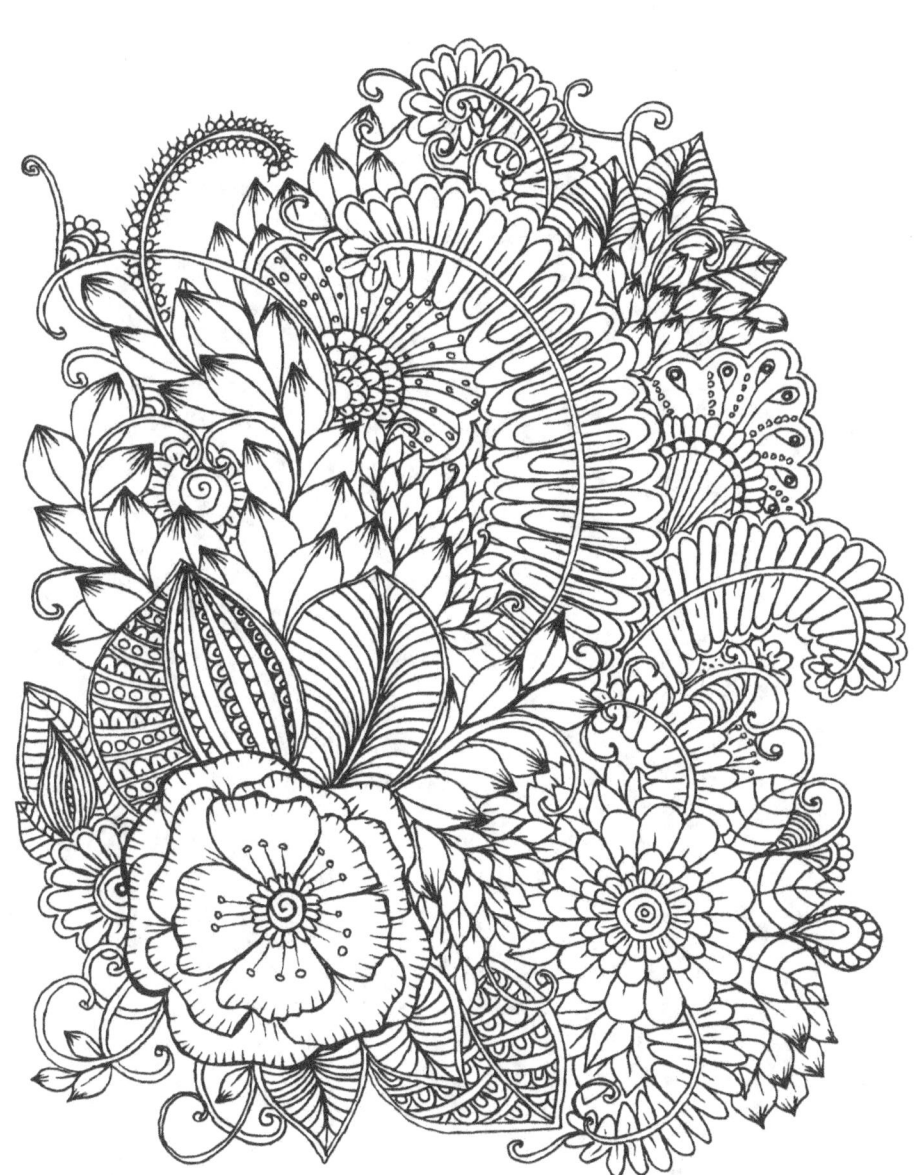

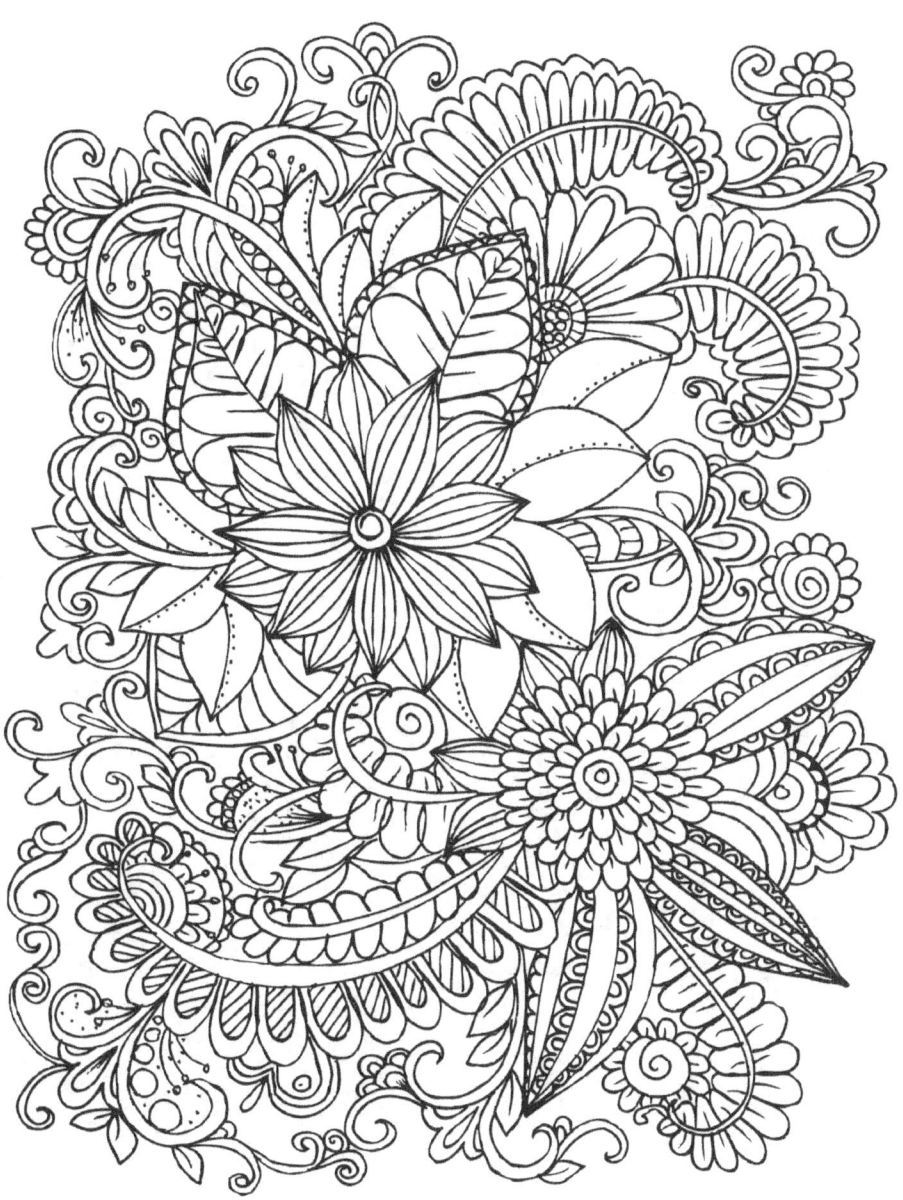

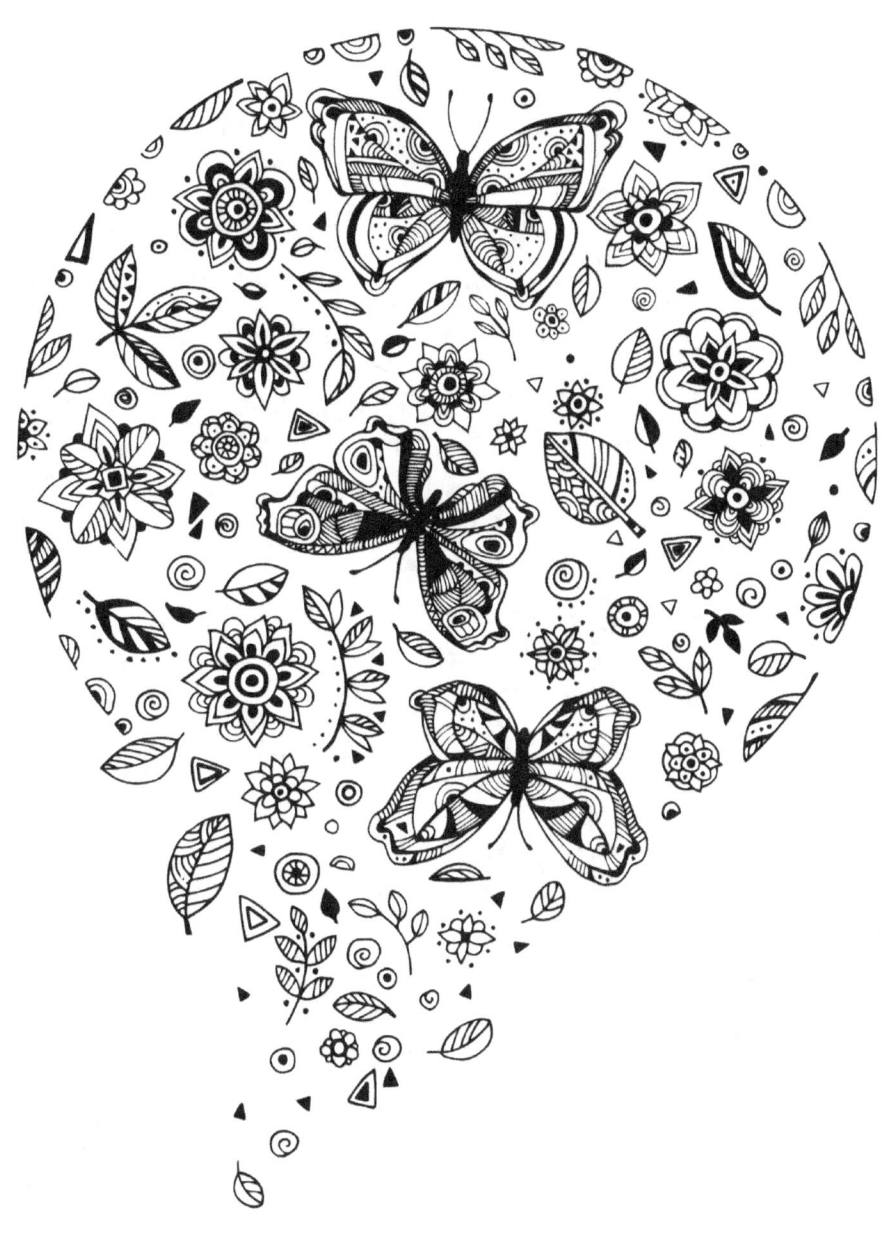

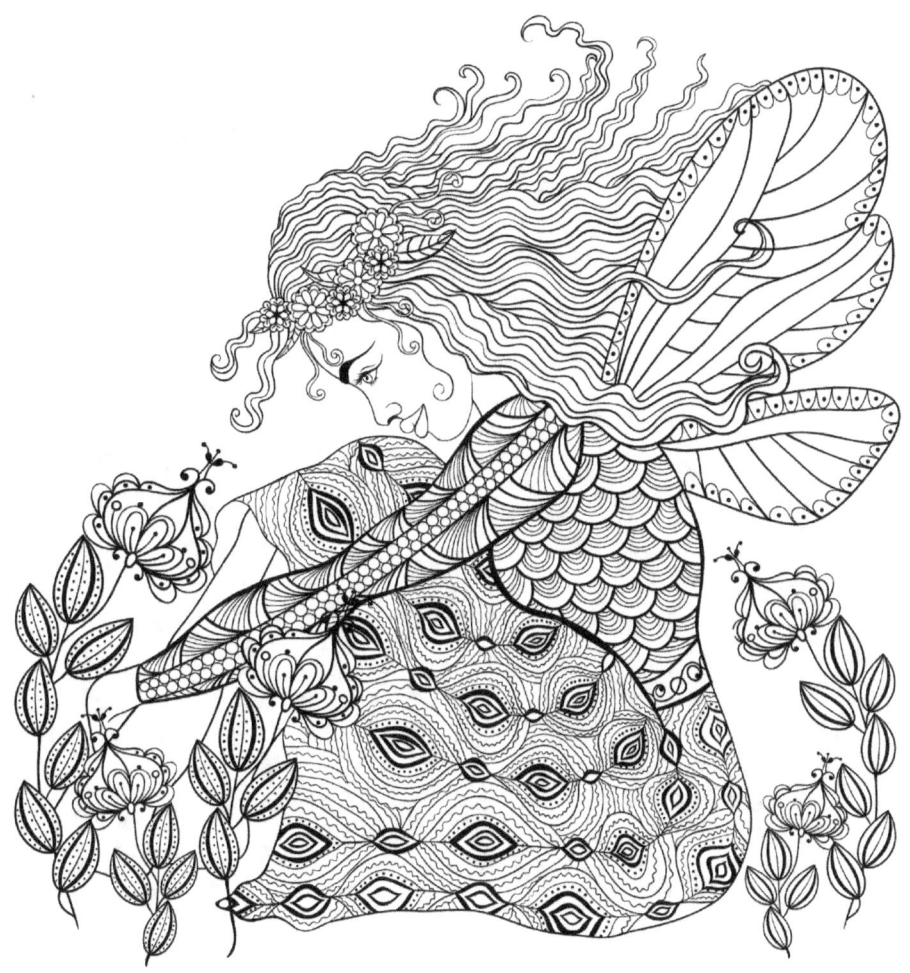

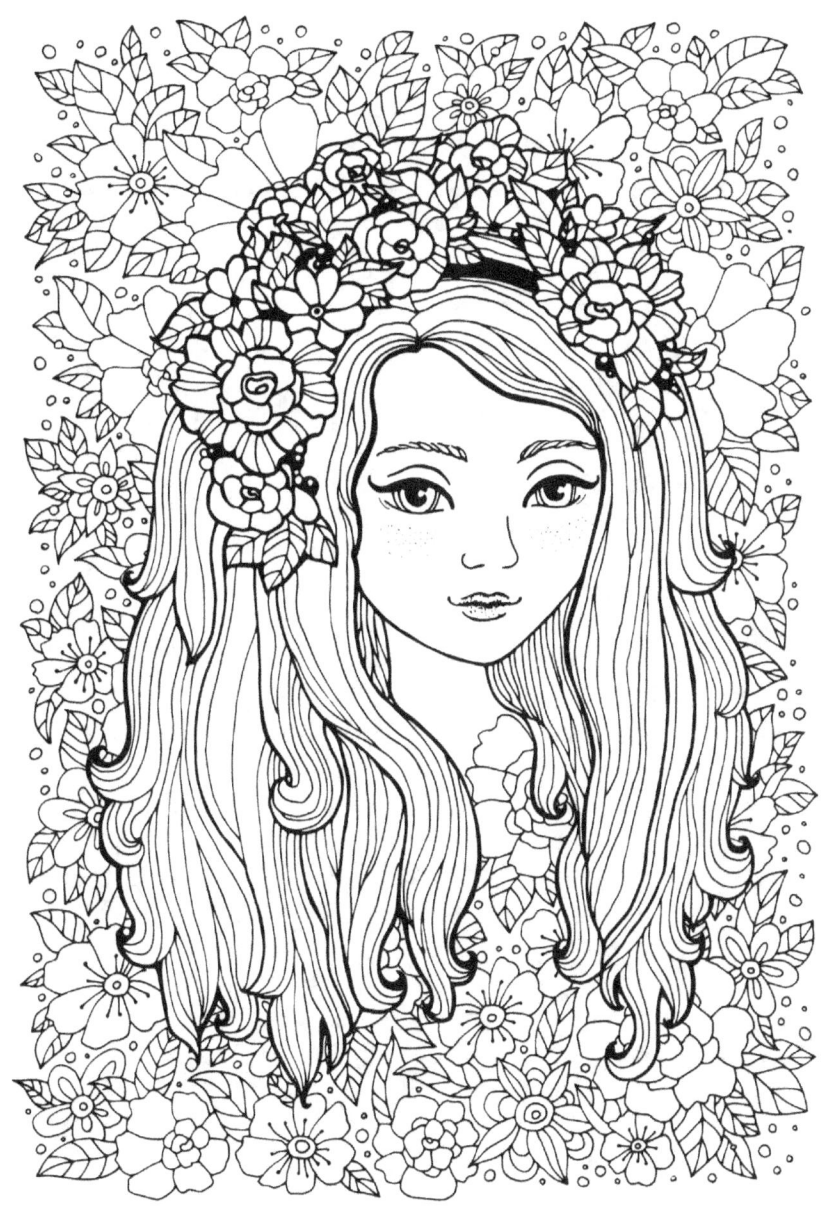

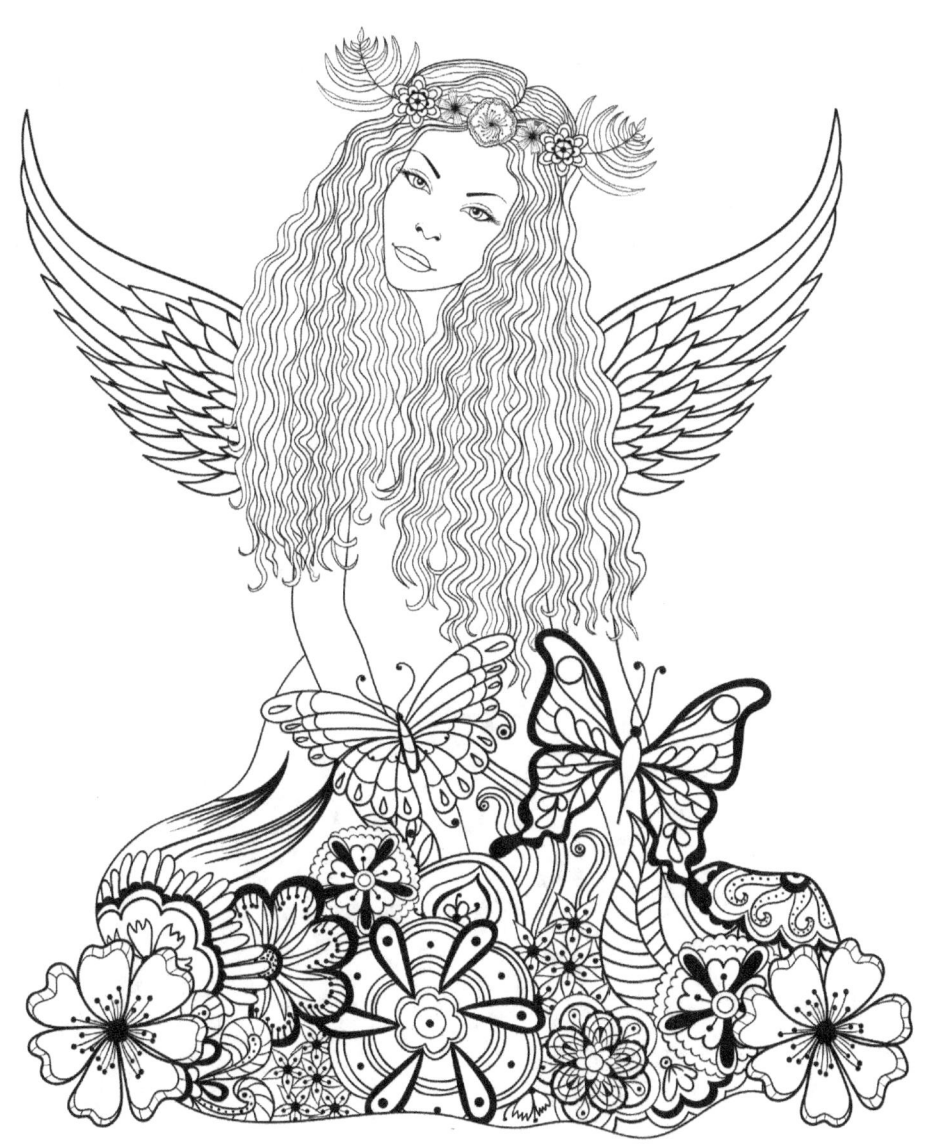

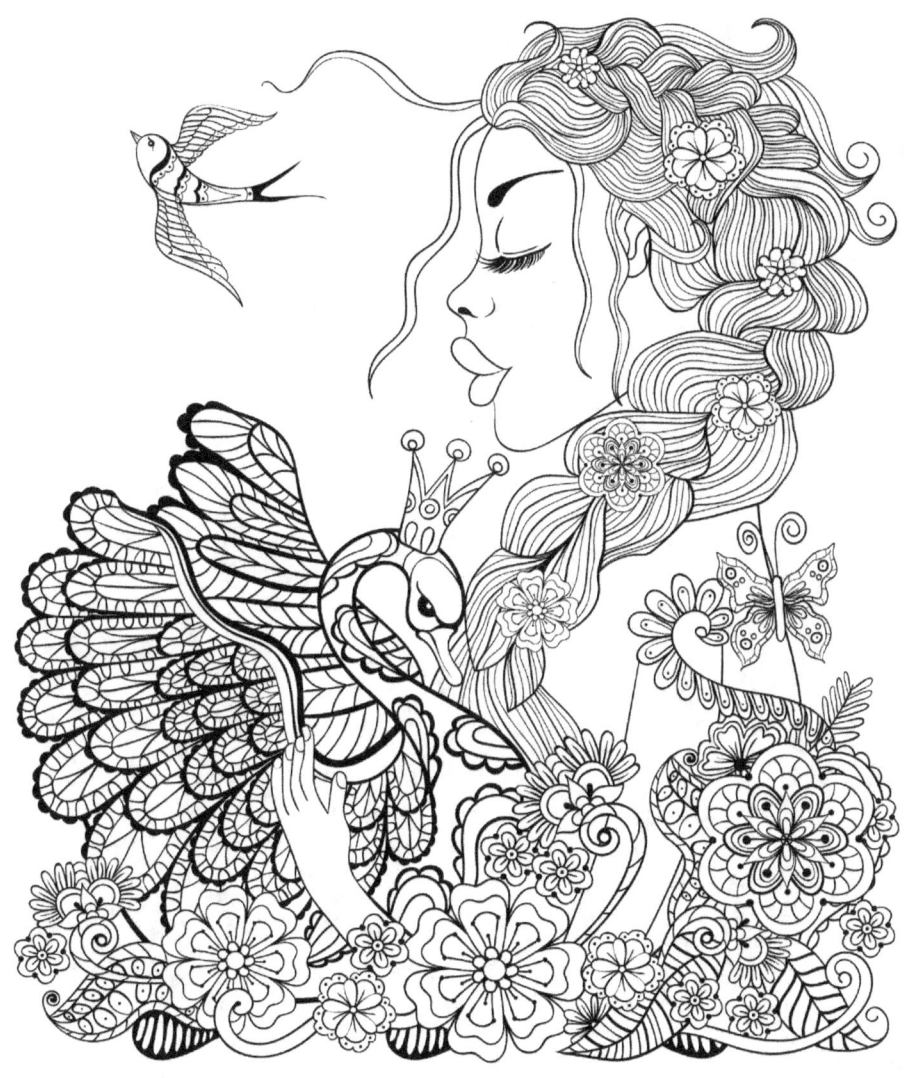

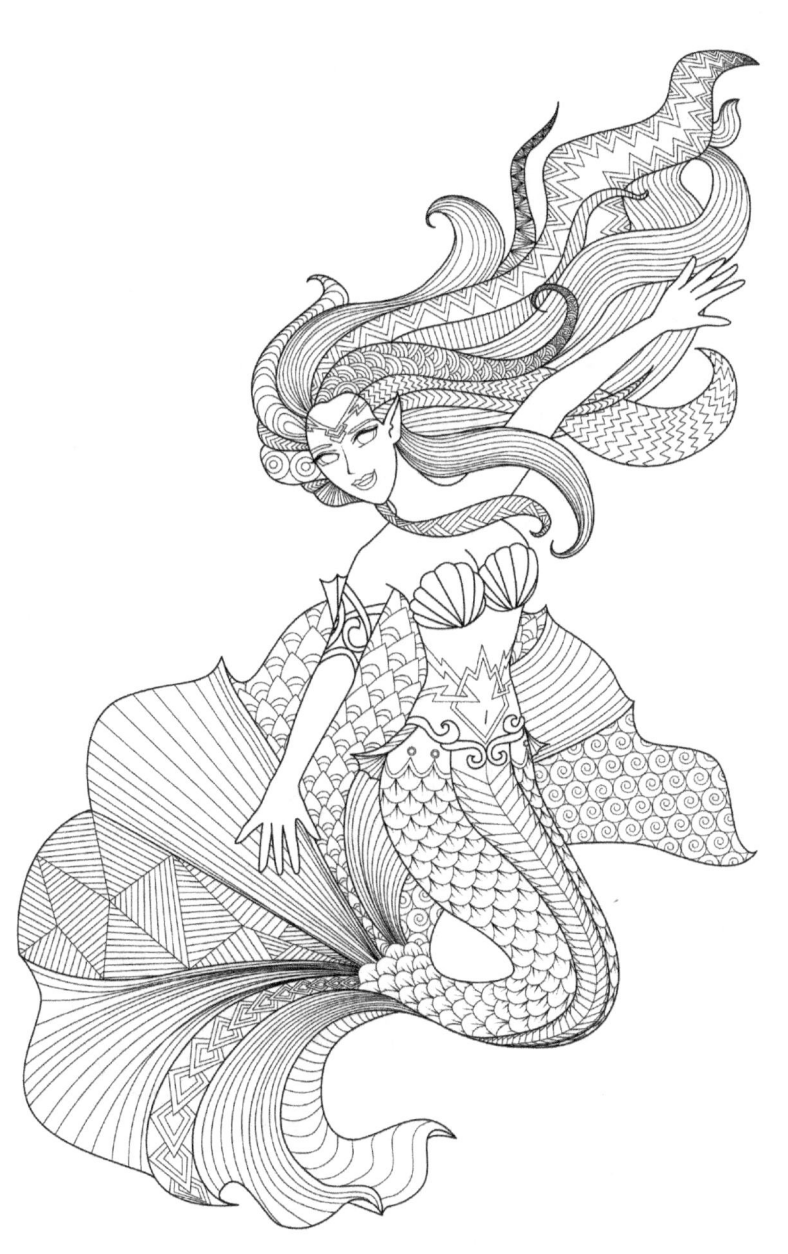

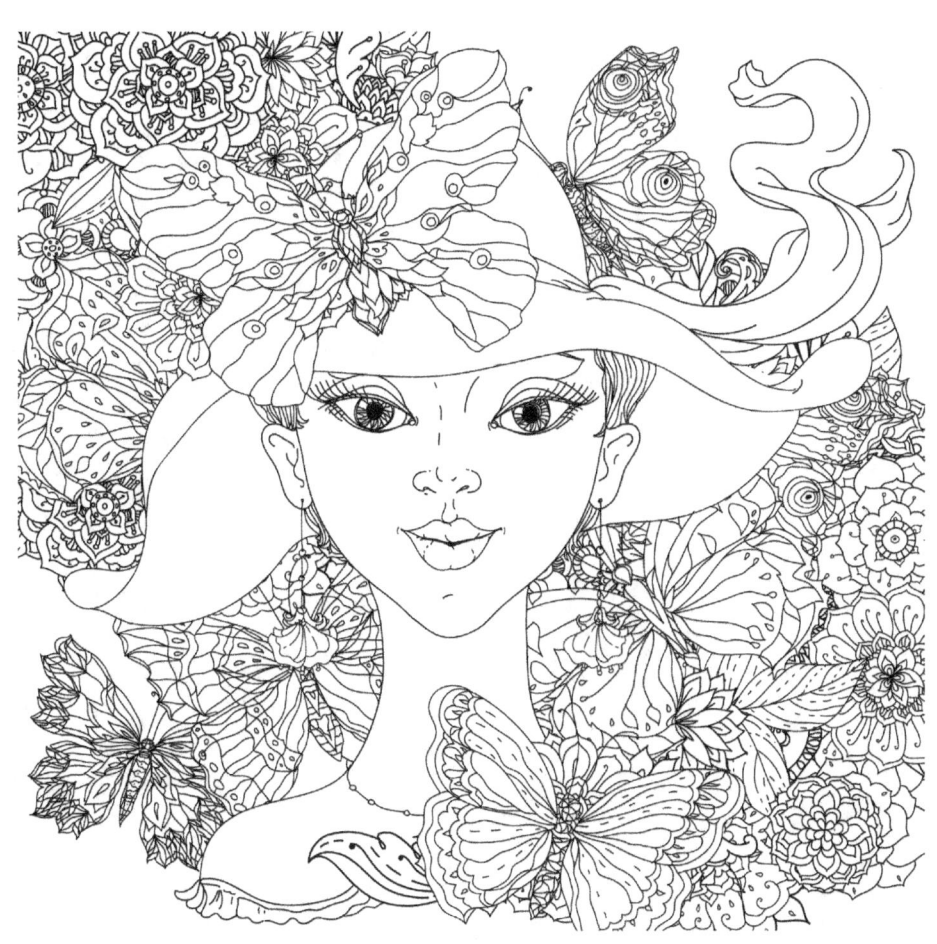

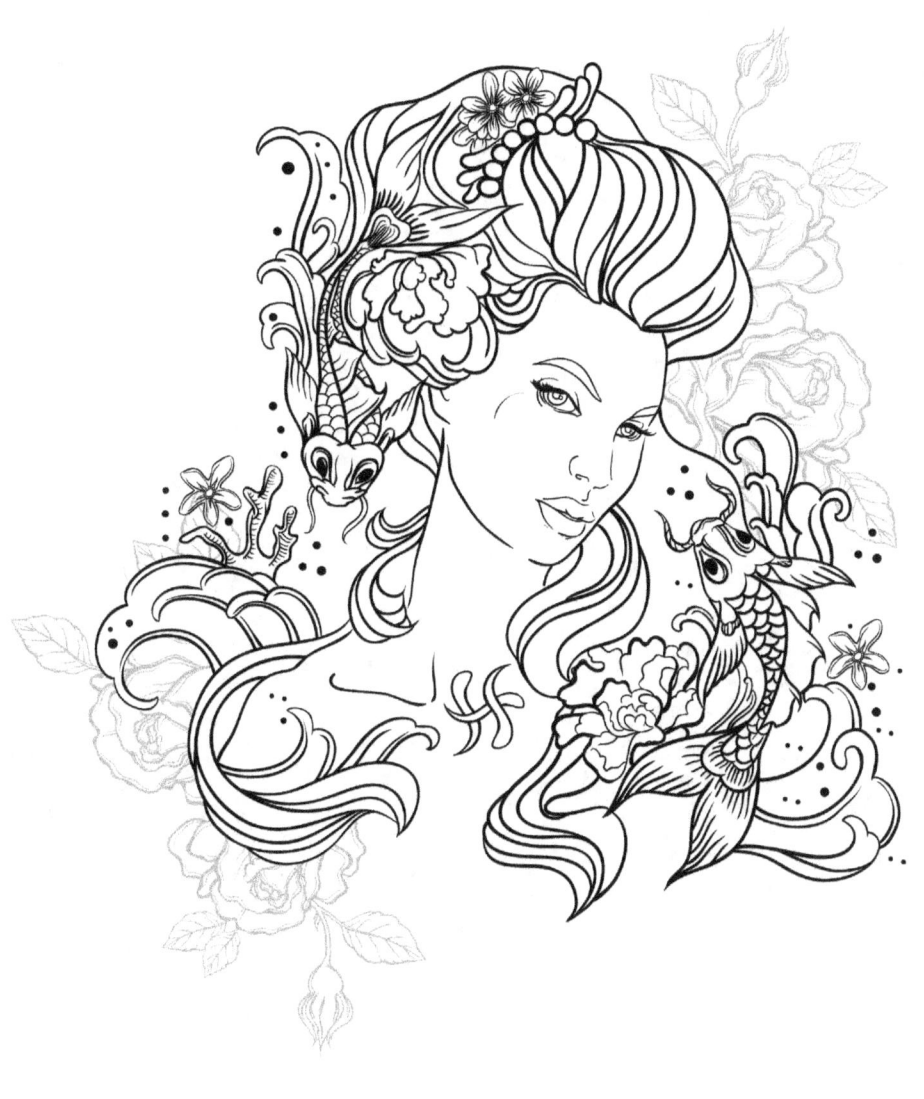

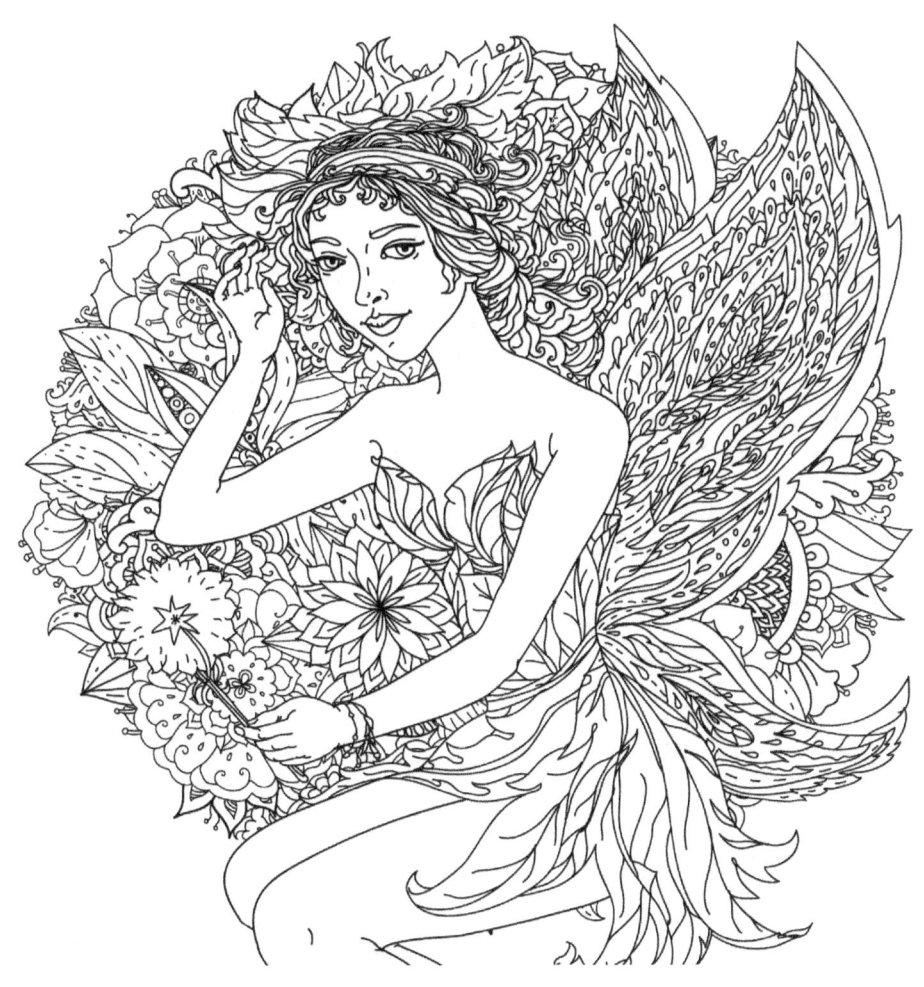

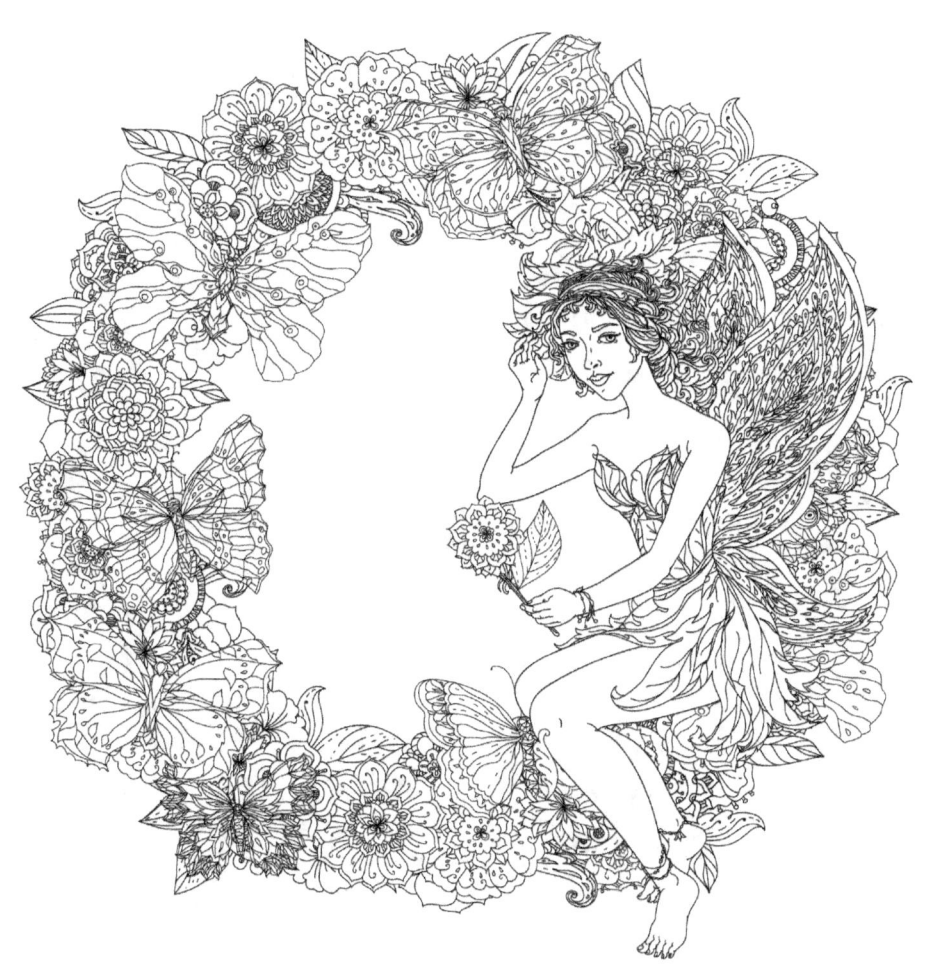

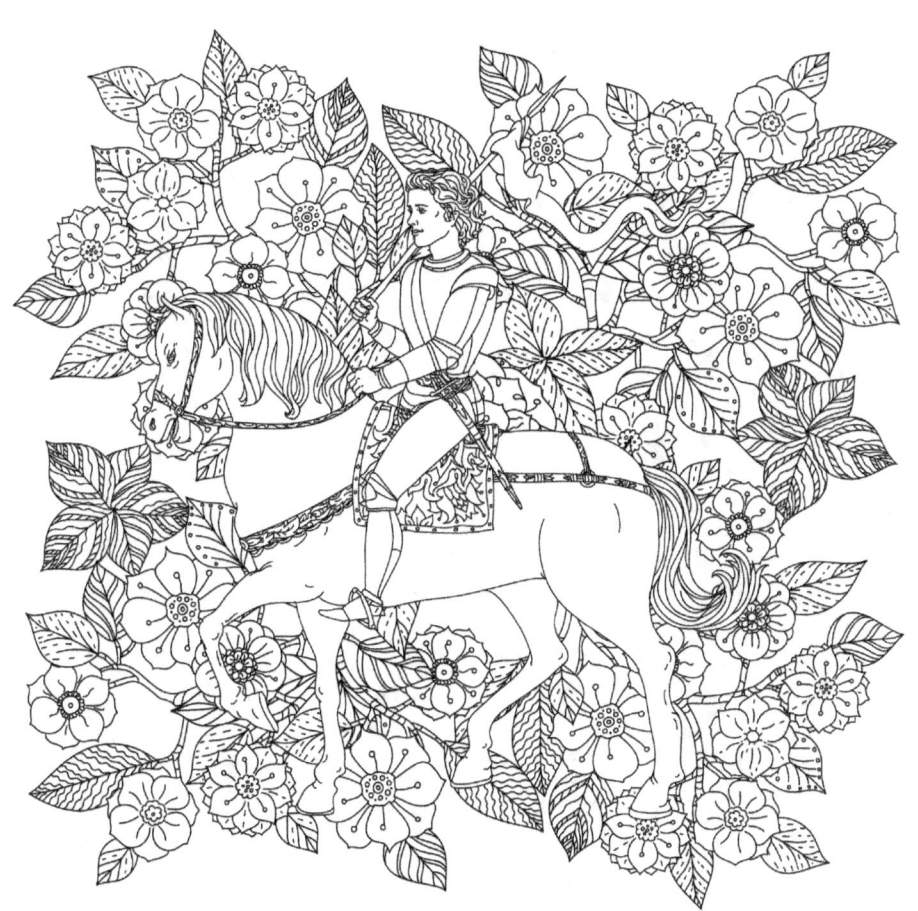

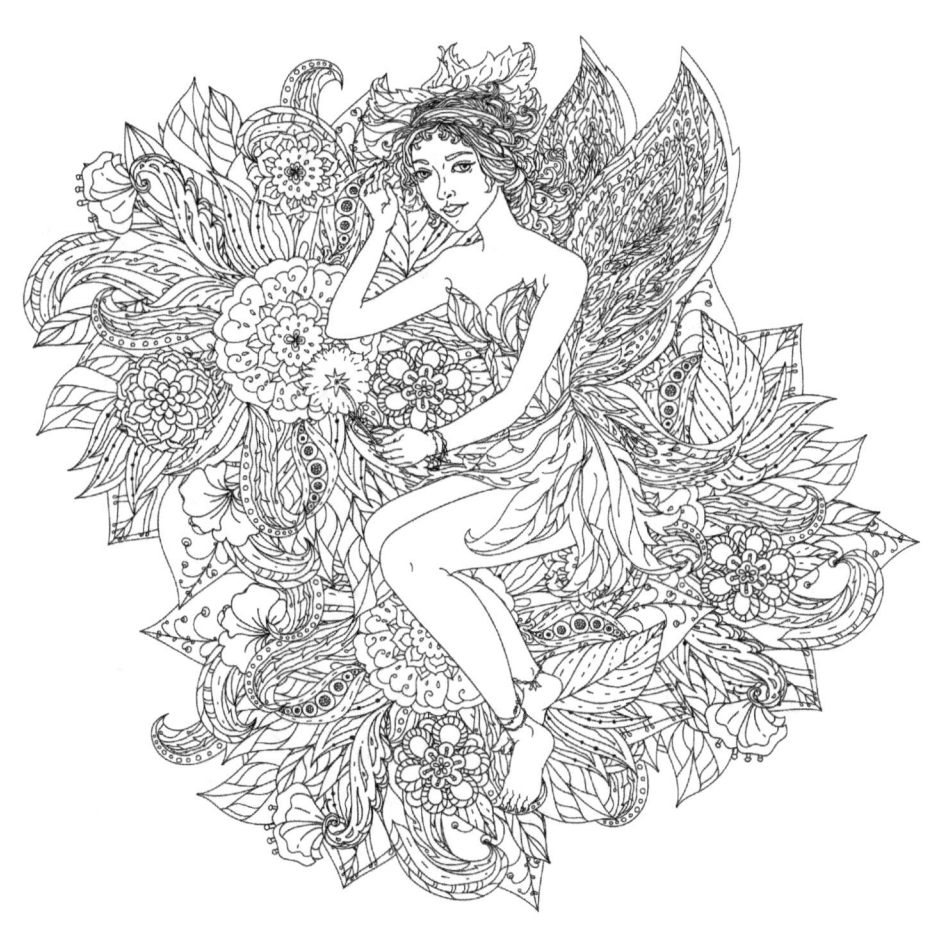

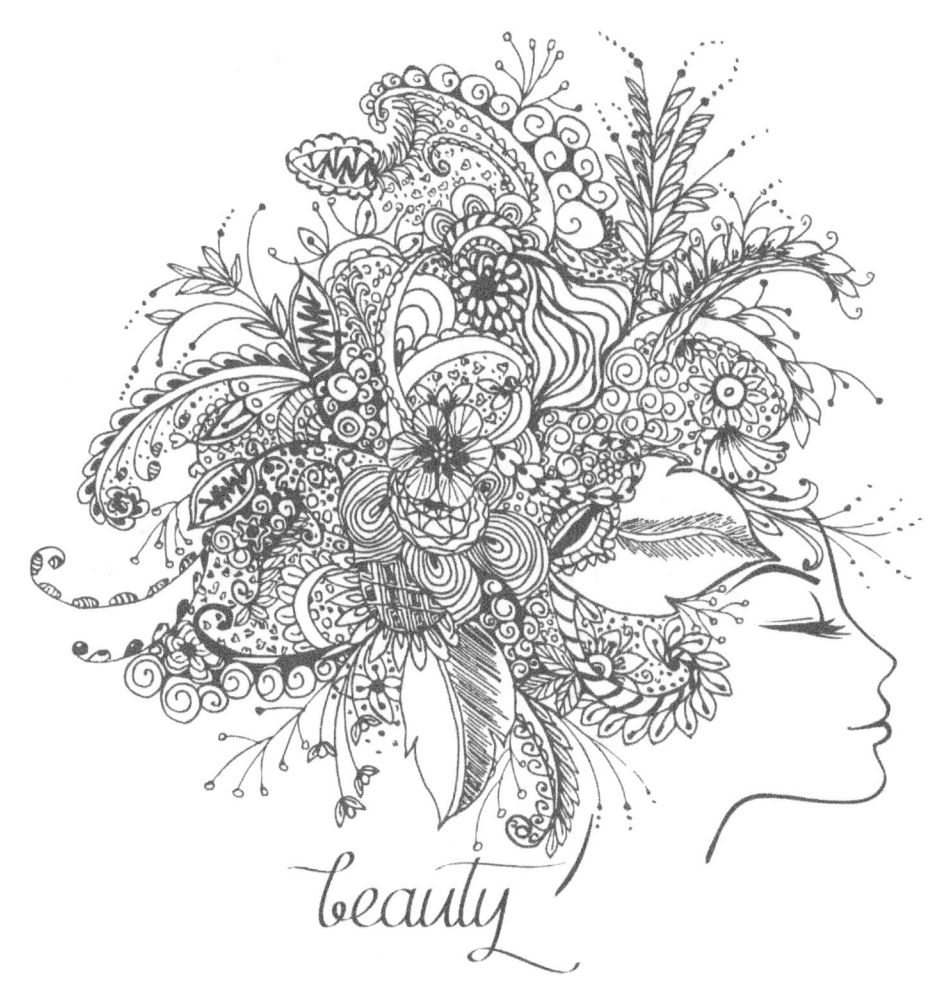

beauty

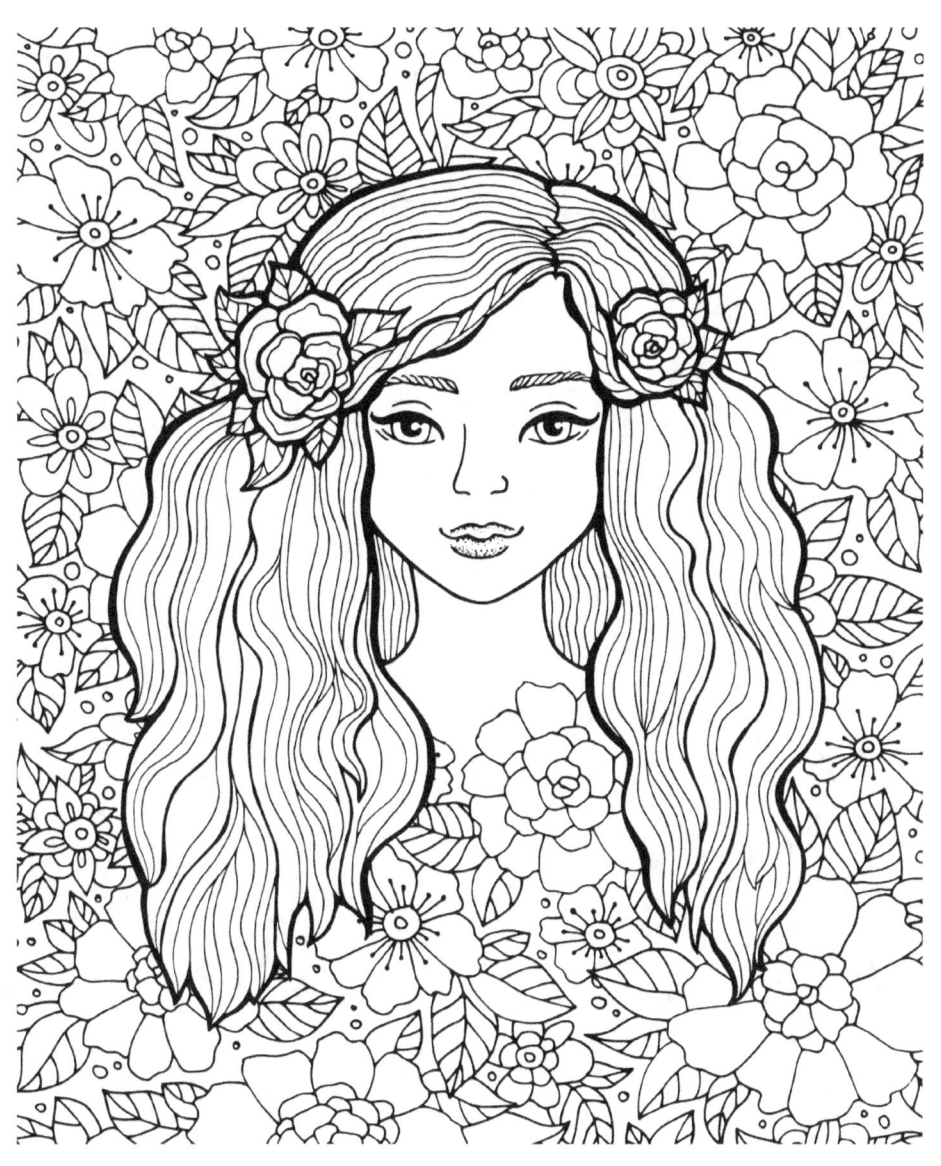

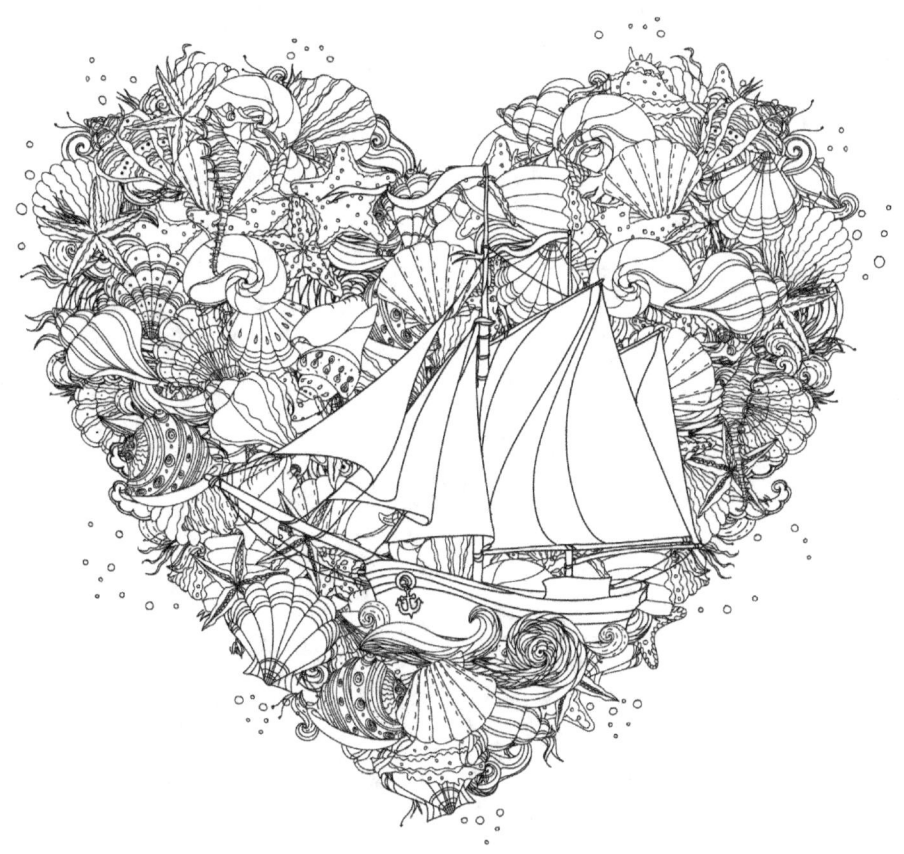

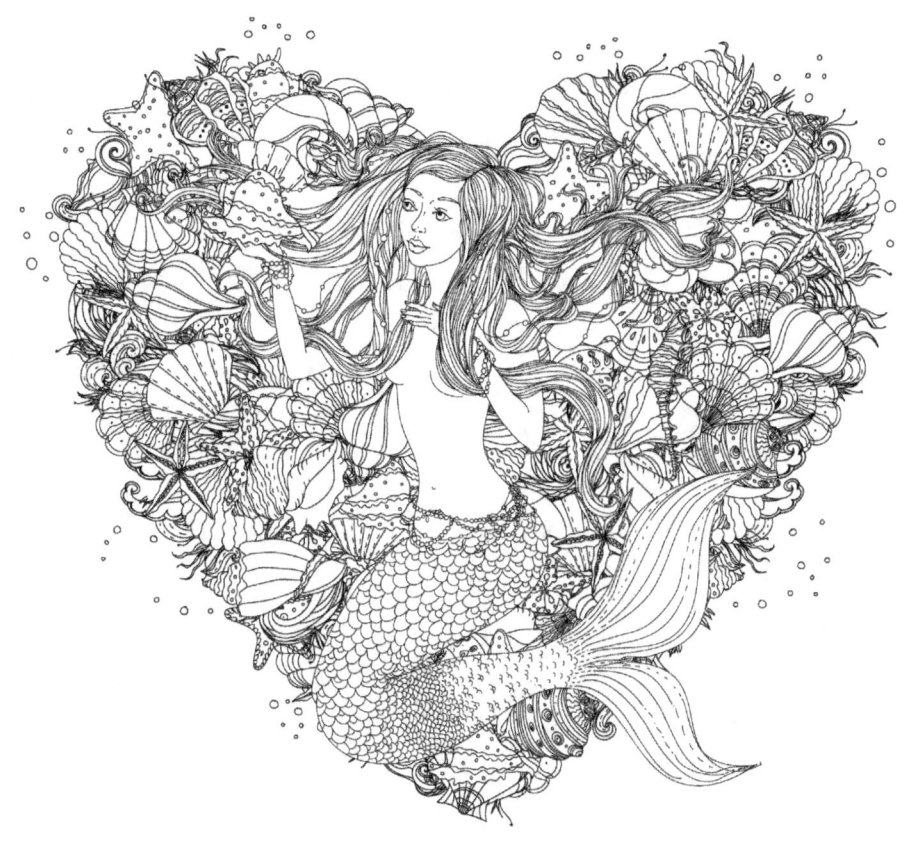

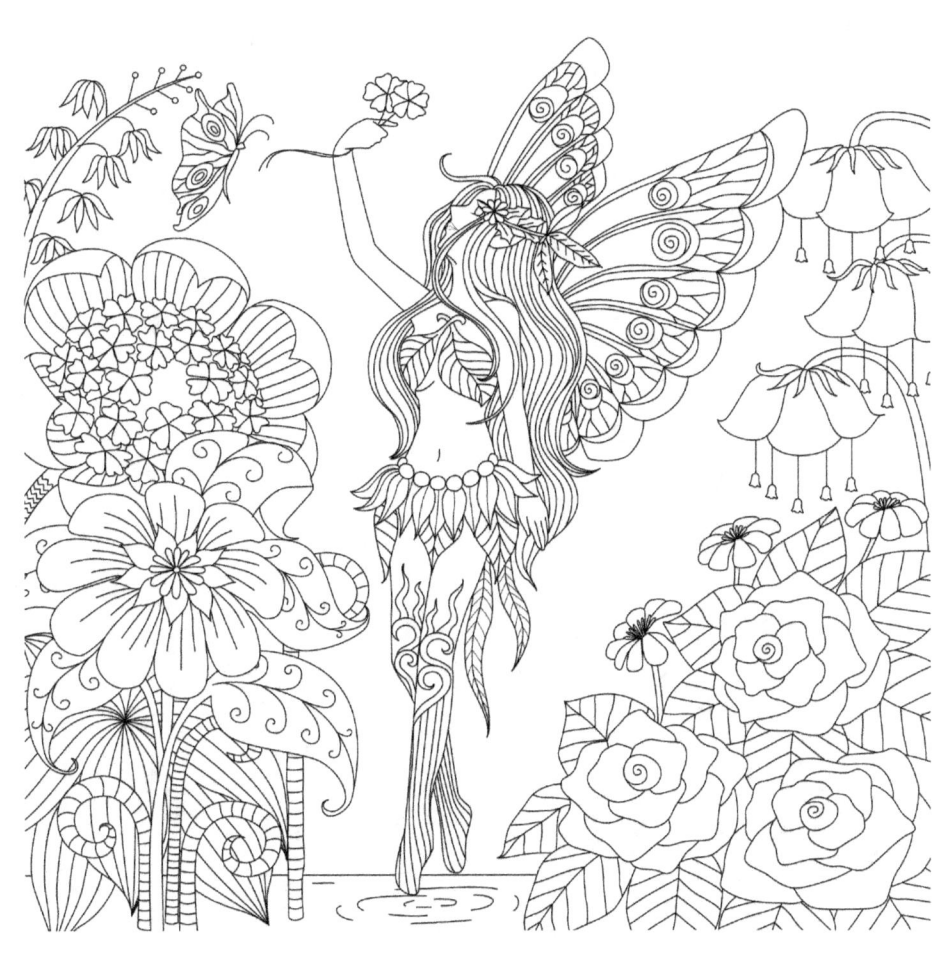

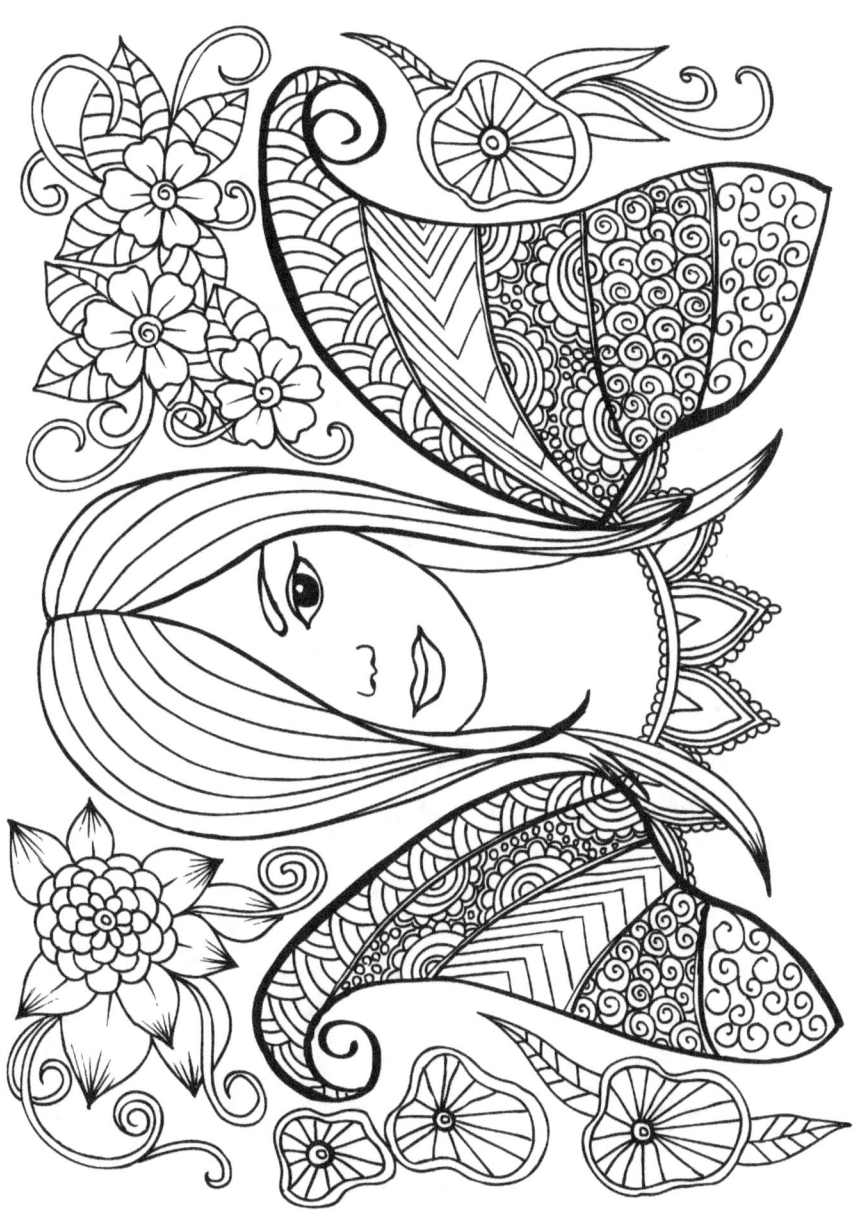

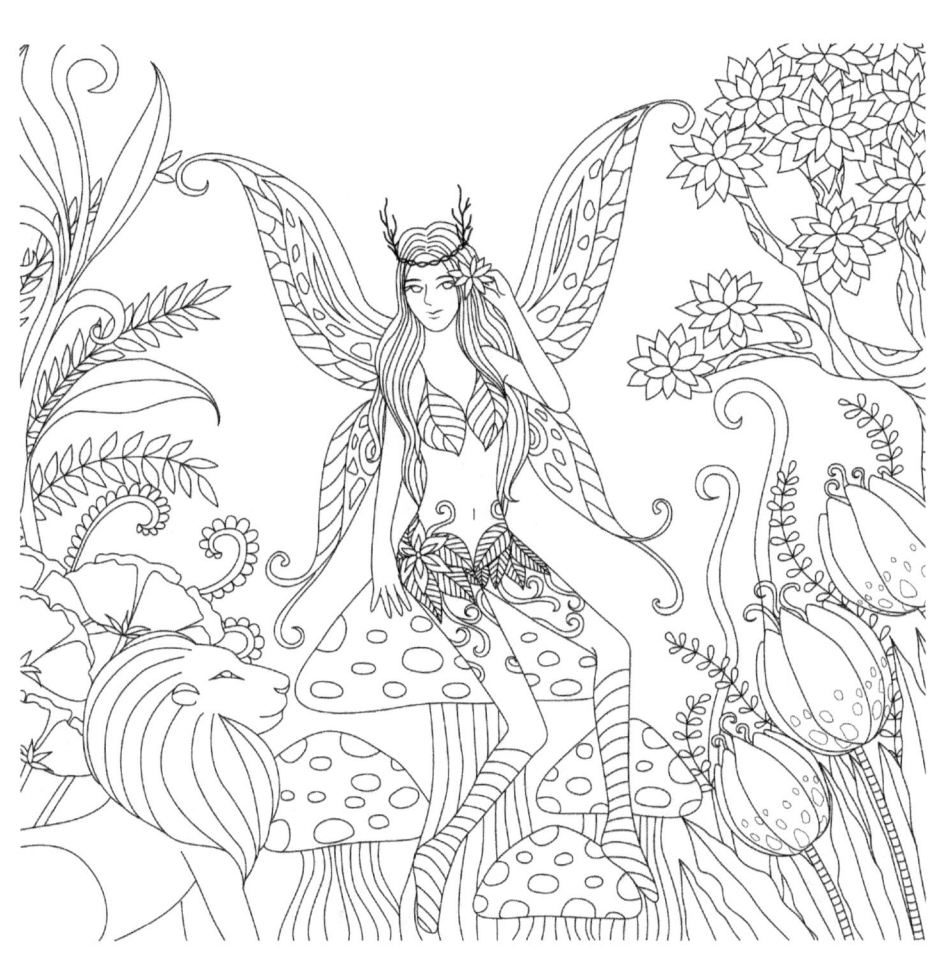

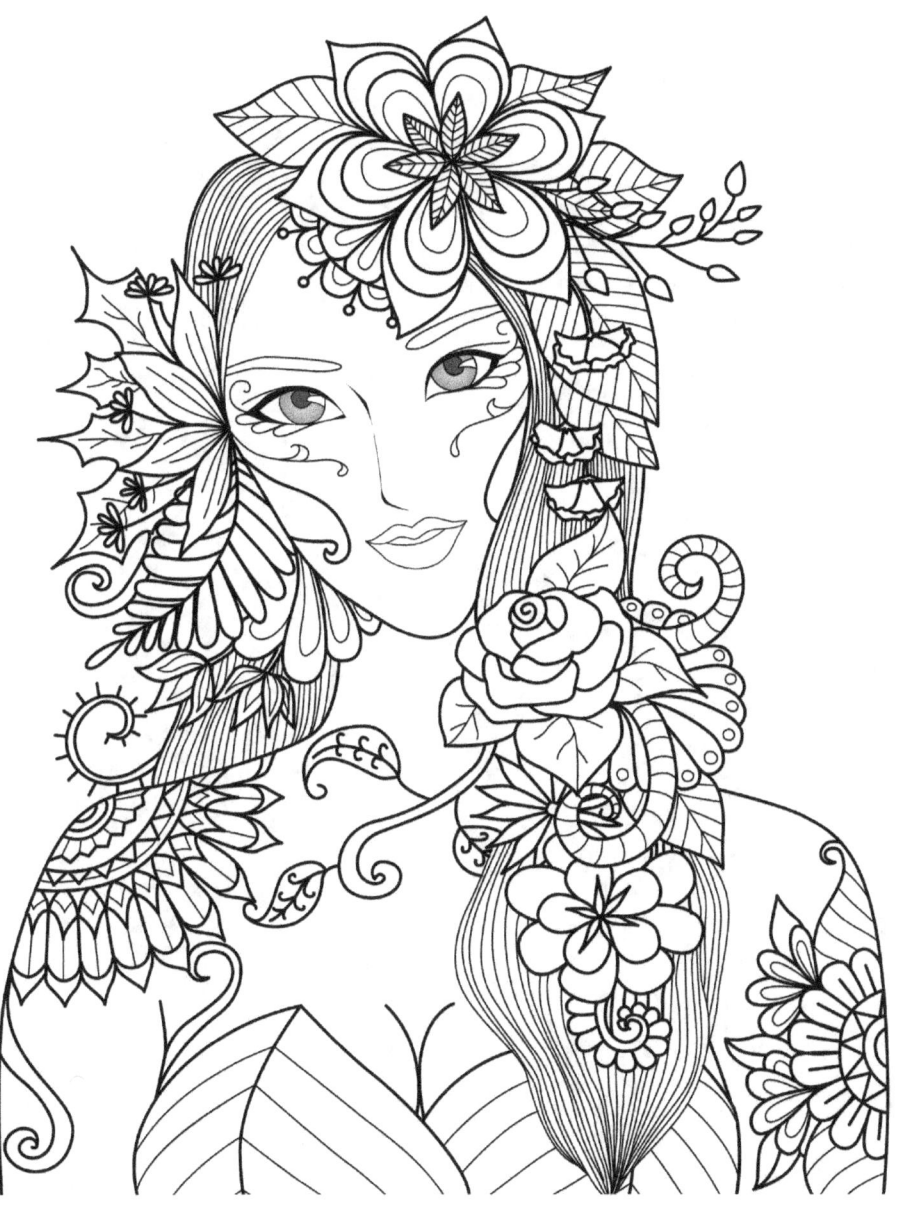

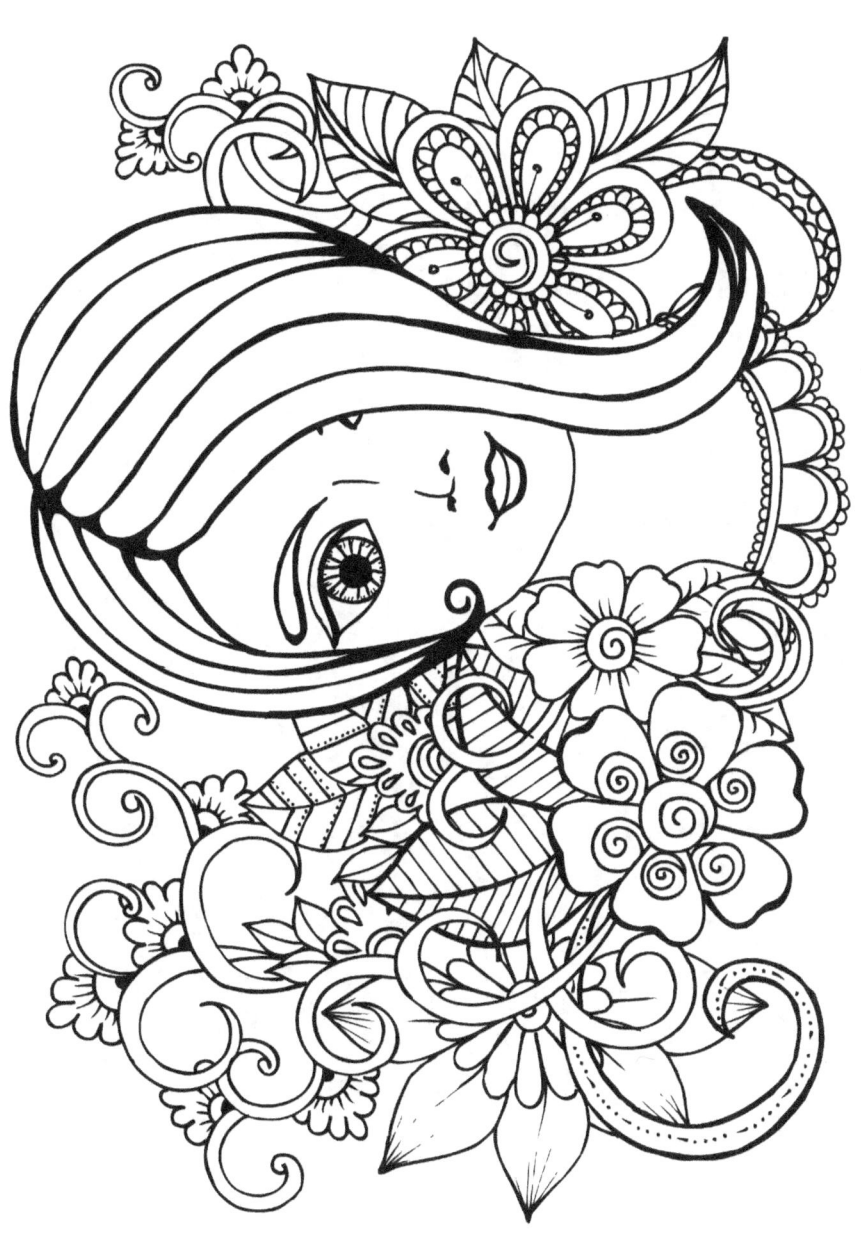

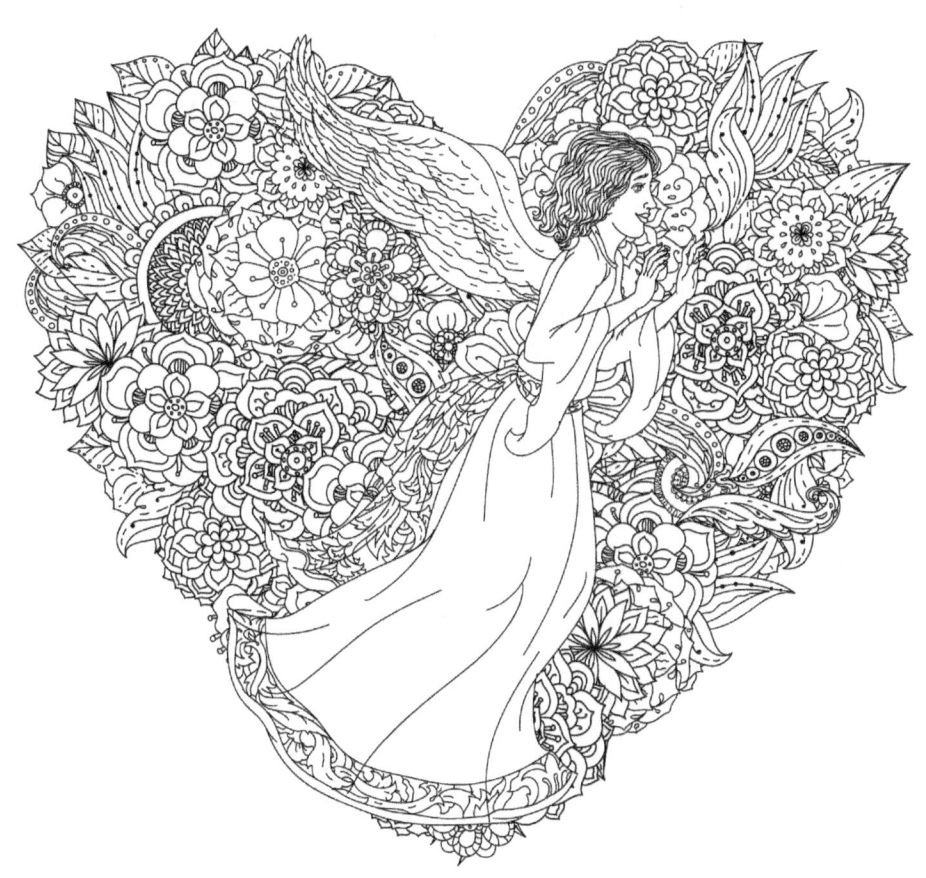

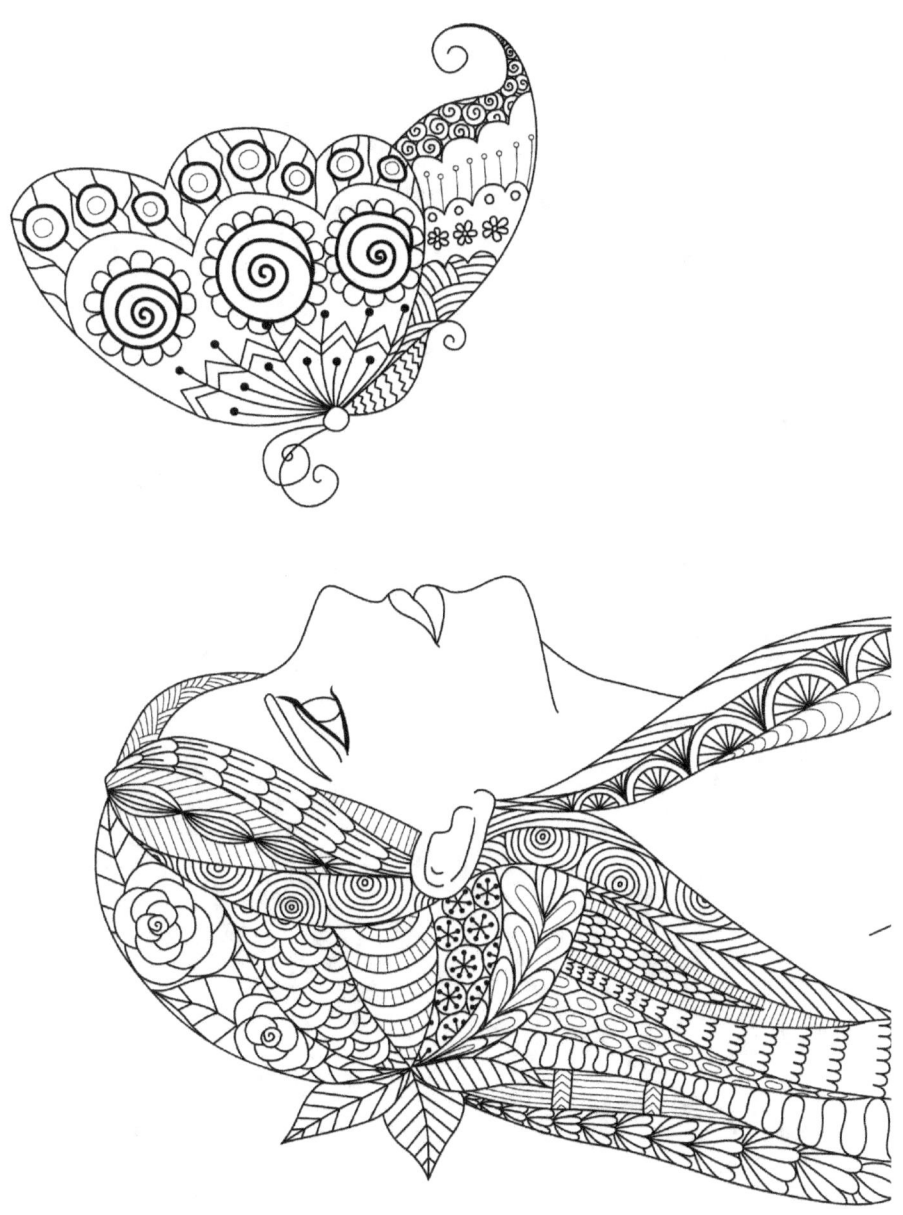

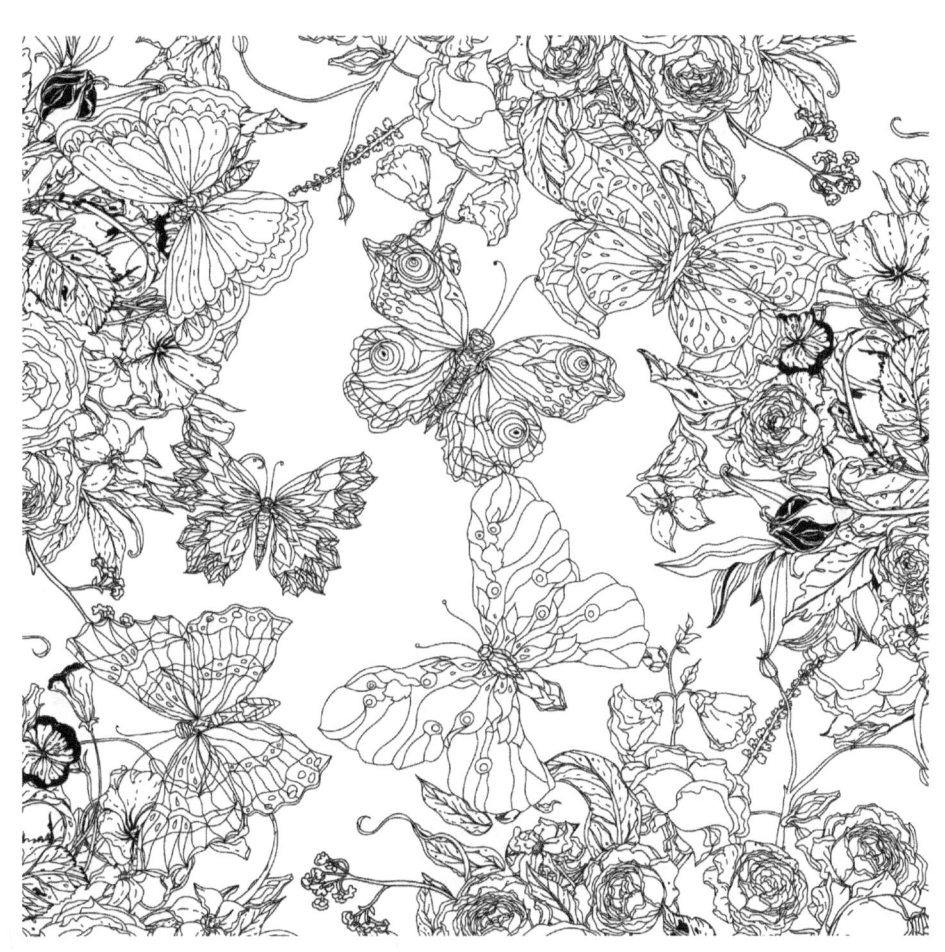

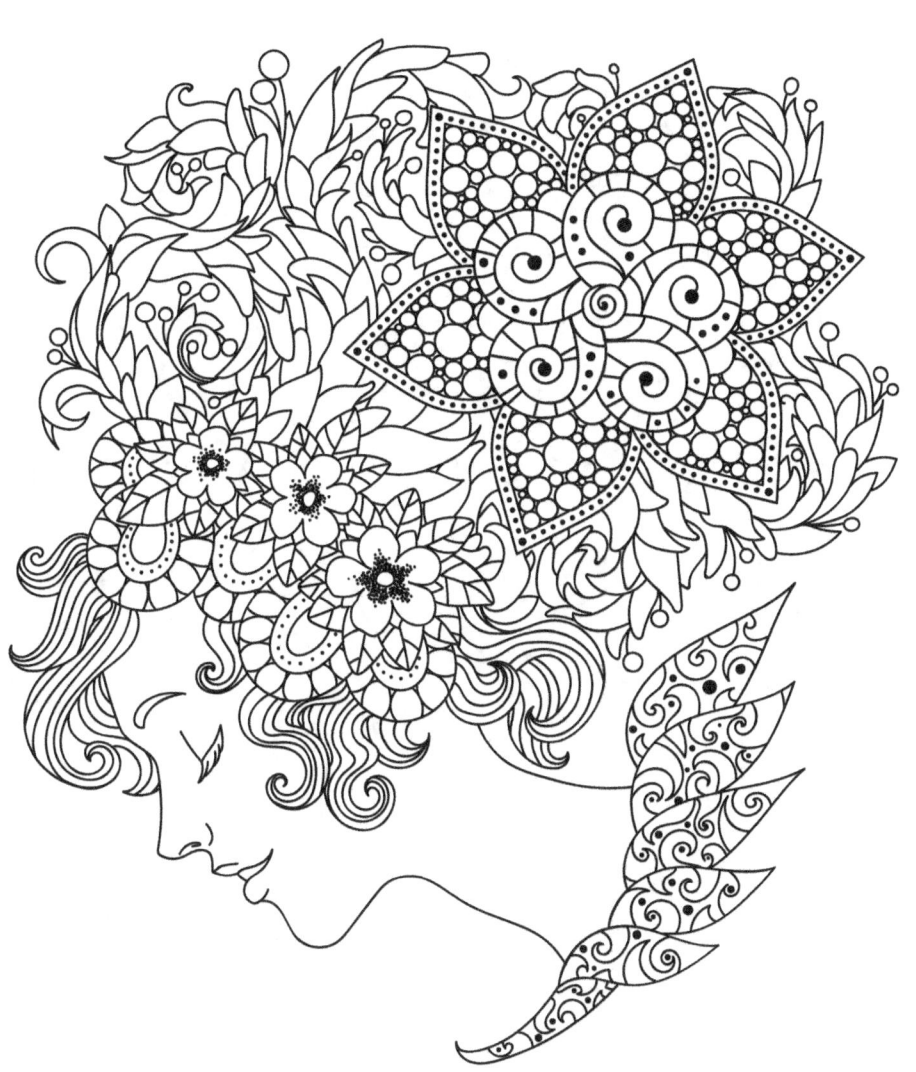

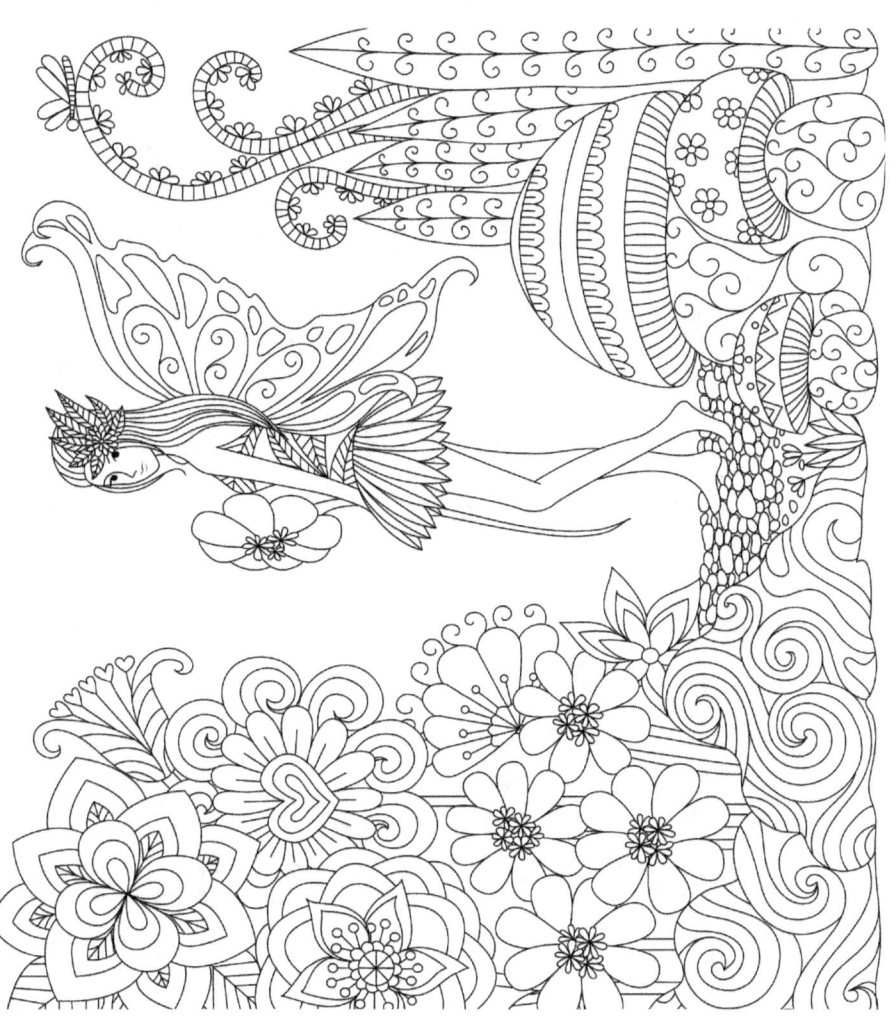

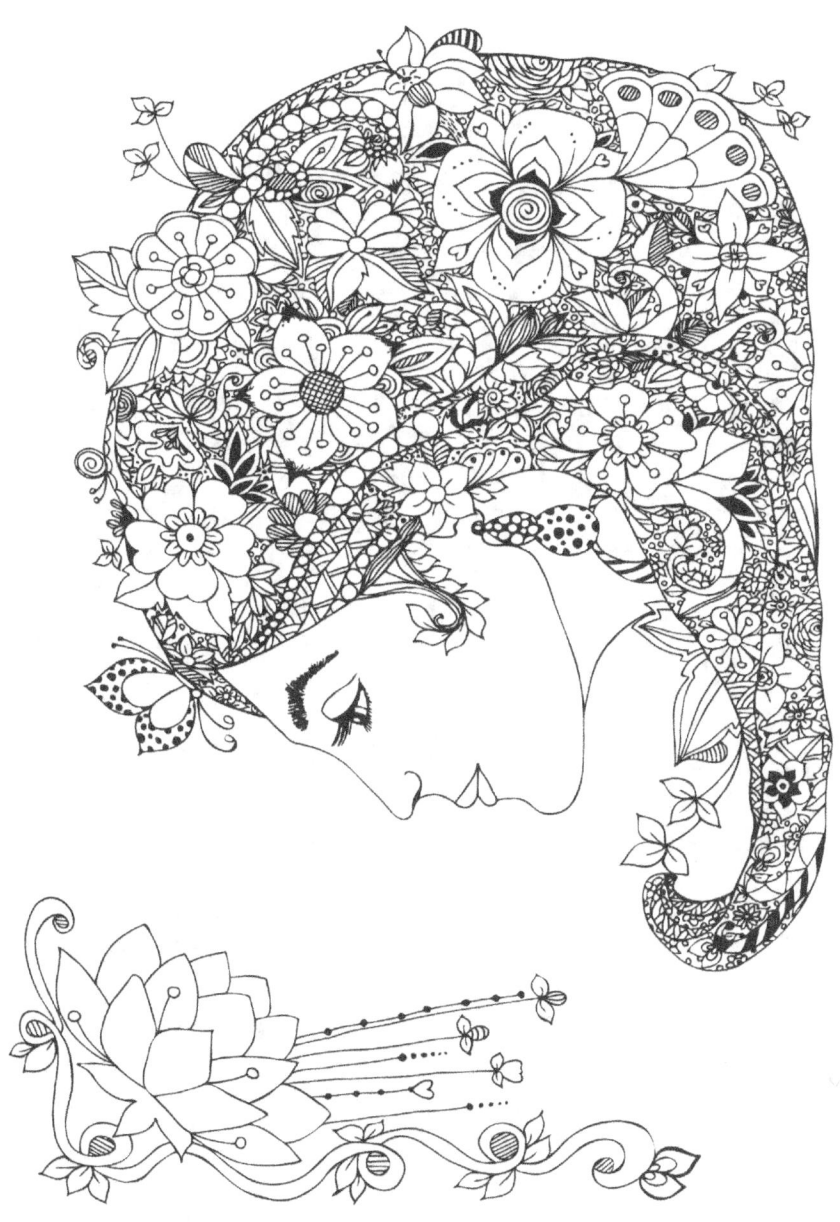

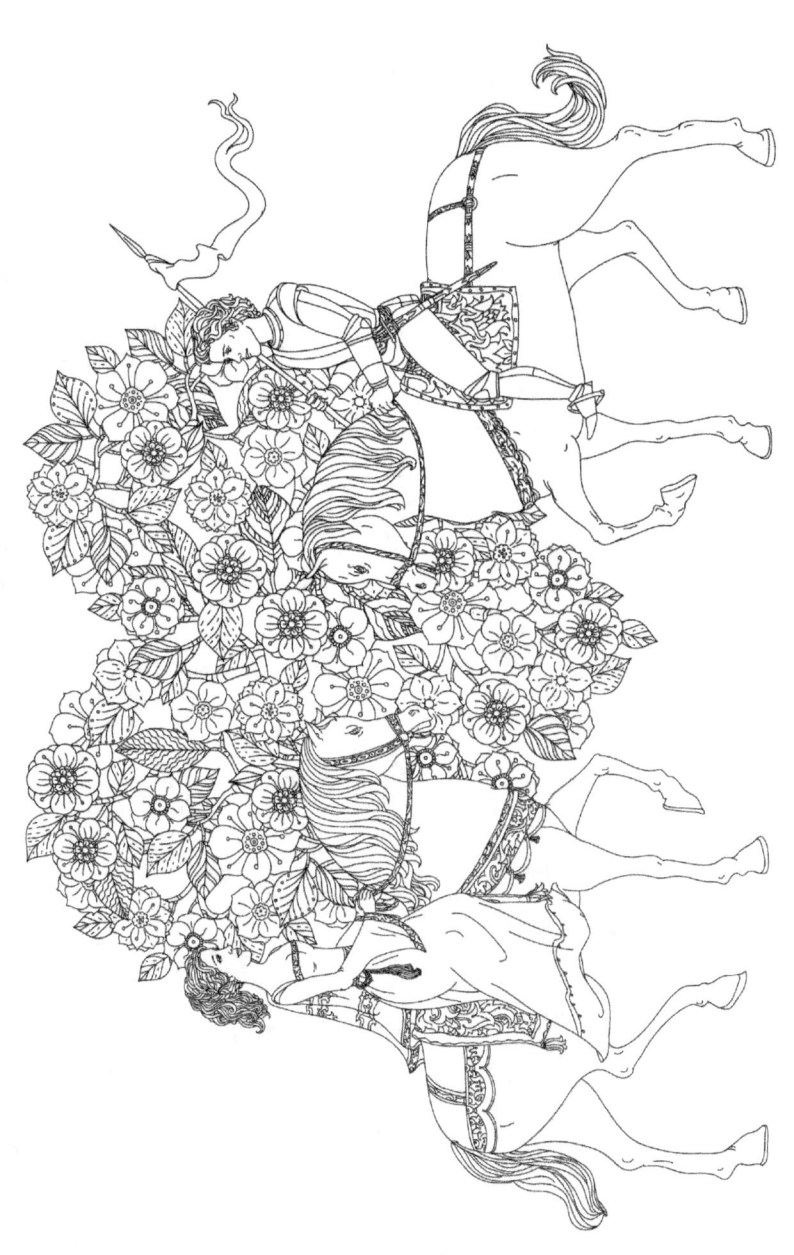

www.ingramcontent.com/pod-product-compliance
Lightning Source LLC
Chambersburg PA
CBHW030035230526
45472CB00002B/515